Saving Democracy from the Populists

Dr Paul Harvey

Clink
Street

Published by Clink Street Publishing 2021

Copyright © 2021

First edition.

ISBN: 978-1-913568-88-7 paperback
978-1-913568-89-4 ebook

Contents

Spiralling Out of Control   1

Why a Grand Strategy?   26

Magna Carta: The Rule of Law   32

A Revolution of Democracy   41

Universal Human Rights   54

Equality and Social Justice   59

Opportunity and Economic Security   66

Environmental Sustainability   75

Conclusion:
The Future of Liberal Democracy   80

Spiralling Out of Control

In 2020 we marked the 75th Anniversary of the end of the Second World War. This in many 'liberal academics' eyes was an ushering in of Liberal Democratic institutions and reconstruction both politically and physically of the shattered post-war world. We might argue that today, 76 years on, Liberal Democratic politics throughout the world has been in retreat in the face of popular right wing nationalism. Retreat, we might suggest, since the American invasion of Iraq in 2003, or it may even be argued that 9/11 was the punctuating point. We can discuss points in history over the last 30 years that define the post-Cold War period, but our argument is essentially that since the turn of the 21st century the post-Cold War Liberal Democratic 'victory' in 1989 has ended with the 'West', in so many different ways, squandering the opportunity that it was presented with, let alone undermining the world system of institutions established in the aftermath of the Second World War.

These are controversial and debatable assertions, not least because having expressed them, the fact that 76 years on since the end of the Second World War we have not seen a war on a global scale like it, is in part a counterpoint to the argument that Liberal Democracy has failed. For all its momentary fury in Vietnam or Afghanistan, wars that were both horrific in their own important ways, the Cold War was essentially as its name suggests and therefore when the Berlin Wall came down in 1989 we might say it marked the end of nearly a hundred years of history. What a brave new world we faced in 1989.

I was at school studying for my GCSEs in 1989 and the profound moment in history was not lost on my generation. That break from the pattern of great power rivalry and the victory of Western Liberal Democracy, as it was perceived by academics like Fukuyama, was a reflective moment in our lives. That's why in such a visceral way the betrayal of that optimism, the misplaced faith in unfettered neoliberal market capitalism and the moralising that followed the fall of the Berlin Wall seems so much truer in 2021 with the benefit of hindsight.

In the last ten years or so, since the economic 'crash' of 2008, we have seen a period punctuated by a battle over 'globalism' between and within countries around the planet. The *Cambridge Dictionary* defines Globalism as:

> *"The idea that events in one country cannot be separated from those in another and that economic and foreign policy should be planned in an international way."*[1]

Gideon Rachman writing in the *Financial Times* (*FT*) in October 2018 suggests a very important distinction:

> *"The difference between globalisation and globalism might seem obscure and unimportant, but it matters. Globalisation is a word used by economists to describe international flows of trade, investment and people. Globalism is a word used*

---

[1] https://dictionary.cambridge.org/dictionary/english/globalism accessed on 30th July 2020.

by demagogues to suggest that globalisation is not a process but an ideology — an evil plan, pushed by a shadowy crowd of people called "globalists".[2]

Understanding globalisation, Thomas Friedman argues, is crucial to understanding the modern world. Friedman's work on globalisation examines the context of the modern era and suggests that there have been:

"...three great eras of globalisation. The first lasted from 1492 – when Columbus set sail, opening trade between the Old World and the New World – until around 1800. I would call this era Globalisation 1.0.

The second great era, Globalisation 2.0, lasted roughly from 1800 to 2000, interrupted by the Great Depression and World Wars 1 and 2.

...right around the year 2000 we entered a whole new era: Globalisation 3.0. Globalisation is shrinking the world from a size small to a size tiny and flattening the playing field at the same time."[3]

Vincent Cable contends that in the vast and multidisciplinary literature which has grown dramatically over the last 30 years, the term globalisation has become a 'portmanteau', meaning a linguistic blend of description, approval or abuse meaning many different things.[4]

---

[2] https://www.ft.com/content/e4593f96-d937-11e8-ab8e-6be0dcf18713 accessed on 30th July 2020.

[3] Thomas Friedman, *The World is Flat*, paperback edition, Penguin Books, London, 2006.

[4] Vincent Cable MP, Globalisation and Global Governance, The Royal Institute for International Affairs, Chatham House Papers, Chatham House, London, 1999, p. 2.

David Held and Anthony McGrew suggest that:

> *"'No single universally agreed definition of globalization exists. As with all core concepts in the social sciences its precise meaning remains contested. Globalization has been variously conceived as action at a distance; time-space compression; accelerating interdependence; a shrinking world; and, among other concepts, global integration, the reordering of inter-regional power relations, consciousness of the global condition and the intensification of inter-regional interconnectedness."*[5]

It does not matter what level or state, regional or supranational, Held and McGrew are arguing about. It is the relationship between those levels and among the actors operating on those levels that defines the idea of globalisation. Globalisation is about interconnected relationships. Held and McGrew continue to argue:

> *"The phenomenon of globalization – whether real or illusory – has captured the public imagination. In an epoch of profound and unsettling global change, in which traditional ideologies and grand theories appear to offer little purchase on the world, the idea of globalisation has acquired the mantel of the new paradigm...*
>
> *But it was not until the 1960s and early 1970s that the term 'globalization' was actually used."*[6]

They look at a 'golden age' of rapidly expanding political and economic interdependence that challenged the traditional

---

[5] David Held, Anthony McGrew, *The Global Transformations Reader*, Polity Press & Blackwell Publishers Ltd, Oxford, 2000, p. 3.
[6] Ibid. Held. Page 1.

separation of external and internal, domestic and foreign, affairs. They describe the growing interconnectedness of modern society as defining the idea of globalisation.[7]

From a religious point of view the Rev. Robert Sirico wrote about globalisation as a phenomenon:

> *"The technological revolution and social dimensions of modernity have made this increased interconnectedness possible. Advancements in technology have made quick and radical improvements in communication and transportation capabilities. The social dimension of modernity contributes the assertion that because all men and women are equally valuable, they should be free from unfulfilling constraints imposed by other persons or the state. These technological capacities and the freedom to develop and use them promise to enhance the potential for integral human development by promoting authentic development in at least the areas of economics, politics, and culture"*[8]

The overlap with technology and its impact in the modern era on society is emphasised by Sirico. It is the all-encompassing nature of these concepts that makes any clear and agreed definition almost impossible. Different academics see globalisation from so many differing perspectives. Jean-Luc Blondel, writing in the *International Review of the Red Cross*, argues:

> *"Globalization is both a fact of life, principally in economics, technology and communication, and an international view of the world. It needs to be considered in terms of its inherent*

---

[7] Op.cit. Held. Page 1.

[8] Robert Sirico, 'The Phenomenon of Globalisation', *Acton Institute*, Volume 12, Number 5, September and October 2002.

> *ambivalence and contradictions: it can, for instance, pro-*
> *mote cultural and scientific exchange, but it also facilitates*
> *coordination between criminal organizations; through the*
> *dissemination of human rights it may help to give greater*
> *freedom, but may also destroy cultures or inflict damage on*
> *traditional economies."*[9]

Globalisation is the interconnectedness of modern societies and individuals in different forms of group, such as the state, the multi-national company, the pressure group, the religious group, the community. How people choose to interact with others reflects a dimension of globalisation. Friedman's analysis is helpful in that it challenges how people relate to each other and how the communication information age has altered the relationship of the individual to the state and government.

The debates about globalisation attempt to define and grasp the meaning of change over the last 30 years. It is the attempt to categorise and analyse the post-Cold War world and early part of this new century that leads to new theories about what is perceived to be occurring. It also reflects the insecurity and the security, depending on the perspective taken, that defines the context of the post-Cold War era and the early part of this new century. People can see globalisation as a positive reflection of society and its strengths in the 21st century, the liberal perspective; or, as a threat that challenges the security of the individual, the community and the state, the populist perspective.

The implications of all of this for Liberal Democracy have

---

[9] Jean Luc Blondel, 'Globalization: Introduction to the phenomenon and its implications for humanitarian action', International Review of the Red Cross, No 855, September 2004, p. 493–504.

been profound, not least because Liberal Democracies have struggled to offer solutions to the social, political and economic challenges we have faced created by 'globalisation' and mainstream governments been accused of promoting 'globalism' at the expense of their populations.

Rachman also identifies:

> *"It is not just the radical right that attacks globalisation as an elite project. Many on the left have long argued that the international trading system is designed by the rich and harms ordinary people."*[10]

The end of the Cold War in 1989 ushered in a period of hope and renewal, just as the end of the Second World War reset the world order in new systems and institutions. That post-Cold War period was shattered by the events of 9/11 and America's headlong descent into the subsequent Iraq War. These key events coupled with the Arab Spring uprisings, the growing power of China and the economic decline of Western global predominance, which was itself shattered by the crash of 2008, has all transformed our political and global environment. It might be reasonable to say that the Liberal Democratic hope of people stood atop the Berlin Wall in 1989 looks very different today in a very different world.

There is a need now more than ever to reassess the situation and define a new 'Grand Strategy' for Liberal Democracy. One rooted in the values and base principles of Western society focused through a re-examination of the ideas contained in the Magna Carta, the American Constitution,

---

[10] https://www.ft.com/content/e4593f96-d937-11e8-ab8e-6be0dcf18713 accessed on 30th July 2020.

embedded in British Rule of Law and representative democracy, as well as universal human rights – there is a need, we might argue, to rediscover the radicalism of these values interpreted in the modern context to guide us looking forward. To re-establish a Liberal Democratic Grand Strategy fit for our age. We are not talking about purely British values, these ideas are not the property of any nation state, but the ideas we will explore should underpin a renewal in Britain of our Liberal Democracy and that in the current crises in politics, health, economics, world security and environmental catastrophe is fundamental.

We will explore six principles that we argue should underpin a renewal of Liberal Democracy:

1. The Rule of Law
2. Democracy and Subsidiarity
3. Universal Rights and Freedoms
4. Equality and Social Justice
5. Opportunity and Economic Security
6. Environmental Sustainability

This is a battle to redefine Liberal Democracy, to use the base ideas to generate a new contract between people. The issue is not that Liberal Democracy has failed, it would be an introspective self-indulgence to try and save the post Second World War Liberal Democratic world as we have known it. Those that have tried to hold on to what was once predominant have failed. The Social-Liberal elites of Western democracies have become disconnected and lack credibility. The defeat of Hillary Clinton and of Gordon Brown was more profound than merely politicians losing elections. They lost the battle to forces which further undermined the 'progress' society has made since the Second

World War. Having tried to tame the neoliberal economic beast unleashed in the 1970s they were consumed by it and became the footnote to the ultimate debasement of the post Second World War era of 'progress' embodied by the election of Donald Trump in 2016. Whether we discuss 'culture wars', 'austerity', or 'identity politics' – proponents of Liberal Democracy must address the future not the past. Therefore, the documents we refer to, Magna Carta or the European Convention on Human Rights (ECHR), are not in-of-themselves the answer, it's the ideas they contain that need renewing in a modern context to reinvigorate modern 21st century Liberal Democracy.

That America has a new President is not enough. Simply winning an election doesn't change the trajectory of the nation. It doesn't stop the politics of the far-right. America is at a juncture, a waypoint in its history. America has a choice to make beyond simply who is President.

No state or democracy is preordained to last forever, but the greatest democratic experiment is crying out for renewal, for a sense of identity in the 21st Century. Founded on the idealism of liberal radicals 245 years ago, America deserves to be understood.

America needs to face its demons and move forward confident in its own self-awareness. It needs to put the Trump years behind it as the aberration it was.

This is a rallying call to Liberals who cannot sit back now. Now comes the hard part. The ultra-conservatives and white supremacists will circle their wagons, lick their wounds and these populists will come back for another go. The Fox News agenda coupled with the corrupted Republican Party will do everything they can to derail American democracy.

There has been such a vacuum of leadership that President Biden now has to show his quality, bind the wounds of the nation and work with moderate Republicans and all Democrats.

One of the biggest geopolitical arguments taking place is about the realignment of power in the context of the re-emergence of China and India. The rise of these traditional global powers and their return to global significance against the backdrop of Western decline is a whole theme of International Political study in-of-itself.

For this analysis it is a central point of why redefining Liberal Democracy is so important. It is easy for the Western populists to slip into a diatribe of xenophobia against China and India. That misses the point, the fact that China and India are strong is not straightforwardly a bad thing. It is bad that the 'West' is weak. The 'West' turning to populist leaders like Trump and Johnson is a sign of fear and weakness, that is what any renewal of Liberal Democracy has to deal with.

The 'West' must be confident if it is to meet the challenge of China, drawing them into a relationship of mutual gain not a competitive cold war. Meeting China head-on in a traditional great power rivalry would be a serious risk and miscalculation, when better strategies may be more appropriate. Understanding Chinese strategy and undercutting it with an equally considered approach is required. Proponents of Liberal Democracy need to extol strength in values that draw China into a relationship the Chinese need. We need to understand China in order to better tackle Xi Jinping's authoritarianism.

To paraphrase Edward Luce in his book *The Retreat of Western Liberalism* [11], politics in the 'West' has not been competent at understanding on the one hand the internal political and economic problems presented by the realignment of power in the world, alongside the rise of nationalism and populism, and the way the wider mass populations of the 'West' have been failed while at the same time those same politicians have compounded the problems with policies that perpetuate the decline. To assert failure is again highly contestable given relative affluence in the 'West' set against a global context, but the failure of Western governments perceived by their peoples is an important point we will discuss.

Politics needs both a mainstream left and right perspective, rooted in common agreement about the fundamental values we all share, we argue to establish a new era of 'progress'. The policies of the neoliberals in the late 1970s and 1980s, that resulted in breaking the economic consensus established after the Second World War, they believed would unleash prosperity for all. The Brexiteers and free-marketeers inside the Tory Party and on the far right still hold to the view of the predominance of the free market and how it has never been truly unleashed. They thoroughly misunderstand that unlocking the consensus was not a positive action, it had far reaching consequences beyond purely economics. It began a decline in respect for people and an adoration of capitalism. People were there to serve capitalism in the neoliberal perspective, capitalism was not there to serve people. In the world they unleashed, space was created for the likes of the far right and populists to regain credibility and redefine themselves free from the baggage of the Second World War.

---

[11] Edward Luce, *Retreat of Western Liberalism*, Abacus 2017.

What they unleashed in the 1980s embodied by Thatcher and Reagan, but grew into the Republican and Conservative parties we know today influenced by the likes of UKIP, the Brexit Party, the Tea Party and the Federalists. The far right has found new form and are again politically acceptable which is deeply disturbing given the lessons of history that we mark in this 76th anniversary year of Peace in Europe following the Second World War. The Alt-Right, that has emerged over the last decade, is just as complicated and centrally structureless as the 'left', so it is a terribly difficult thing to explain at the best of times. There is no one Alt-Right or far-right and it would be a major mistake to try and homogenise them.

There is, however, something fundamental going on in society where the 'right' in all its forms has gained and, in some places, succeeded through the democratic process, only to further undermine the democratic process from a position of power. Look at an American election rally for Donald Trump and see people chanting 'Lock her up', or 'Make America Great Again'. Trump, we can argue, sowed social division in such a way that he has undermined democracy in America which is as startling as it is deeply worrying. The Republicans' apparent efforts, we might suggest, to supress voting are thoroughly shocking given the fact they are the party of Abraham Lincoln.

Take the Brexit slogan of 'take back control'. We might even look at Viktor Orbán's Hungarian brand of authoritarianism, or the rise of Auf Deutschland. Each has in different ways connected with people beyond the fringe political movements that spawned them. We could argue that the likes of Farage, Trump, Cummings and Bannon have had a dramatic effect on the Republican and Conservative parties, fuelled by the electorate's disconnection from the institutions and politics of the mainstream.

Edward Luce argues that:

> *"Unlike during the early Industrial Revolution, today's poor are not intentionally displaced. Instead they are being silently priced out of their homes…. More of Britain's poor live in suburbia or 'slumburbia' than in the cities nowadays. This is creating a new kind of poverty, were the poor are increasingly pushed out of sight…. The West's metropolises are in the midst of a grand renaissance. These knowledge hubs and global cities that have more in common with their international counterparts than with their national hinterlands. Anyone who doubted this was disabused in 2016. Almost two thirds of London voted to stay in the European Union. The rest of England and Wales disagreed."*[12]

Inside major powers like France, Germany, America and the UK the questions of what the 'left' and 'right' stand for and how they connect to the world we live in are fundamental. Even deeper are questions about democracy itself and the institutions established in the post-Second World War world which now appear anachronistic in the face of the populist onslaught. The established political order that has held sway for 76 years or more is being challenged as never before by a reactionary populism that has taken over much of the conservative wing of Western politics and sought to recast the political landscape we thought we knew, not just on the right but as a consequence also on the left.

Winston Churchill is often rolled out as the poster hero for British Conservatives. The current Prime Minister

---

[12] Op.cit. Luce p. 46-48.

Boris Johnson, it might be suggested, passes himself off as a 'Churchillian' tribute act, but as with all imitations, his pales in comparison to the original. While Boris was the cheerleader for Brexit and the campaign to leave the European Union draped itself in jingoistic flag-waving nationalism, they missed the fundamental lesson Churchill extolled in post-World War Europe and forget he was a Liberal before he became a Tory:

> *"We must rise to a level higher than the grievous injuries we have suffered or the deep hatreds they have caused. Old feuds must die. Territorial ambitions must be set aside. National rivalries must be confined to the question as to who can render the most distinguished service to the common cause, moreover we must take all necessary steps and particular precautions to make sure that we have the power and the time to carry out this transformation of the western world. Much of this of course belongs to the responsibilities of the chosen governments responsible in so many countries. But we have gathered together at The Hague, to proclaim here and to all the world the mission, the aim and the design of a United Europe, whose moral conceptions will win the respect and gratitude of mankind and whose physical strength will be such that none will dare molest her tranquil sway."*[13]

This is the radicalism we need to rediscover, to make real in people's minds the true context of our modern era, a message that speaks to the issues people face today grounded in the values so eloquently espoused by Churchill. We should acknowledge that Churchill is a highly complex historical figure and his legacy is deeply problematic.

---

[13] Winston Churchill. Europe Unite. Speeches (1947 and 1948). Londres: Cassel and Company Ltd, 1950. p. 318-321.

I was a member of the Labour Party for 25 years, a Labour Councillor for 18 years, twice a Parliamentary candidate and in all those years without fail I pounded the streets door knocking and campaigning for the party and values that I believed in and still do.

Over the last ten years the seeds of Labour's current malaise were sown by Ed Miliband and the subsequent internal party nightmare he was responsible for creating, fulfilled by the Corbynistas who took over the party in 2015. We need to be careful when using the term Corbynista because what do we mean? In this analysis we make the distinction between supporters of Corbyn and Corbynistas, who we define as the core party activists and Corbyn's inner circle. Corbyn, we might argue, gained support for the Labour movement from people who rallied for all their various reasons around his election as party leader in 2015. There was not one single view or platform they endorsed, they were as divided as the wider 'left', indeed the wider 'left' beyond the Labour Party rejected Corbyn. Inside the Party his leadership could be described as 'cult'-like, an adoration of what people each in turn felt he stood for. Anyone who criticised him was hounded and abused with a puritanism and zeal by his devotees.

While Corbyn succeeded in motivating many young people his coalition was unstable because his politics was grounded in a time long before many of his supporters were born. Many young people on the left were Remainers, internationalists more so, and his reticence on Brexit from his own position as a 'Bennite', undermined his appeal. You can chart his decline from 2015 through the failure to connect and cement a place for these young people in the movement, rather his focus we suggest was on old battles.

It is ironic that a group, Labour Together, led by Ed Miliband has conducted a review of the 2019 Election defeat. The report suggests that Labour lost because of Corbyn, but that the roots of defeat go back much further, some 20 years they conclude. The disconnect they propose is between metropolitan Labour and the rest of the country. It might be argued that Labour's defining moment was the election of Ed Miliband as Leader and the party's withdrawal into introspection.

Over the last ten years one of the most powerful, relevant and important democratic socialist movements has been brought to its electoral knees by the Miliband/Corbyn era. The election of Sir Kier Starmer, as Labour leader, is a moment for pause and reflection. This work argues that there is a need to chart a new course, one that sets out a new mission for a modern centre 'left' perspective, relevant to today's 21st century. The term 'left' is packed with value judgements and political philosophical baggage. There is no such thing as 'the left'. The reality is that the myriad of groups, parties and organisations that operate on what they believe and define the 'left' to be are not one homogenous 'left'. Even the Labour Party is still a broad church of views and perspectives, despite the best efforts of the devotees of Corbyn to turn into a church of adoration.

The challenge for those who have a centre left perspective, embodied in the UK by the Labour Party for over a hundred years, is to avoid the battle with the parties internal 'left' wing simply for the soul of the Labour Party. A war over mechanistic control of the party machine will solve nothing and offer little to the people in our country and world that need a new modern centre 'left' capable of challenging and winning power ready to implement a program to transform their lives. Those young people that rallied to Corbyn did so believing Labour was the platform to achieve change. Those on the centre left need to look beyond the Labour Party to reinvigorate politics, they should desire to reclaim the movement not just the machine. Reclaim the substance of what a centre 'left' platform should be both philosophically and in policy. They need to reach past the Corbynista's to those young people, among many groups they need to reach out to, who supported Corbyn to invigorate them with a renewed Labour Party. That inclusive approach also has to reach out far beyond the party and engage communities that have become disengaged with Labour and politics.

Whenever we look to the history of the movement there have always been these underlying tensions between wings and factions. From the origins of the movement with key figures like the Webbs, through Atlee and Bevan, through Gaitskell and Crossland, to Foot and Blair – the traditions within the movement have always experienced tension and transition.

But across Europe and America the 'left' in all its various forms and perspectives has been struggling for relevance. It seems that there is a disconnect between the policies and politics of the representative parties and organisations on the 'left' and the reality of people's lives.

David Goodhart argues in his book *The Road to Somewhere* that "50 years ago, people in leafy North London and people in working-class Northern towns could vote for a Labour Party that broadly encompassed all of their interests. Today their priorities are poles apart." [14] This argument reinforces Luce's point about the divisions we see that go beyond the old party loyalties we have been used to observing. [15] The Guardian published extracts from the 'Labour Together' report led by Ed Miliband, which highlights statistics that reinforce Luce's and Goodhart's analysis. Labour's support is based mainly in metropolitan areas and they lost support beyond those city limits. [16]

The 2019 Labour Manifesto was not 'the longest suicide note in history' as its predecessor in 1983 was described. It was full of policies that alluded to a world no one in reality connected with, understood or recognised. Those promoting it failed to connect with people. They could not get their message across. It was divorced from people's everyday reality and on that basis far worse than its 1983 predecessor. This was the Corbyn perspective unleashed. The December 2019 British General Election was his election. He and the team he built around him lost it in the face of a most incompetent and divided Tory Party, and their response was to suggest it was all down to Brexit, it was not 'they' of course who were the problem, it was the electorate or the media.

Labour lost the 2019 General Election not because of Brexit, although Corbyn's lack of a clear position did not help. Labour lost because people rejected Corbyn and what he stood for. That is a very contestable point and would be hotly debated by many party activists and Corbyn's

---

[14] Goodhart, *Road to Somewhere*, Penguin Books 2017.
https://www.penguin.com.au/books/the-road-to-somewhere-9780141986982 accessed 30th July 2020.
[15] Op.cit. Luce.
[16] Guardian Graphic, source Ian Warren, Centre for Towns 2019 https://www.theguardian.com/politics/2020/jun/18/key-points-from-review-of-2019-labour-election-defeat

supporters, but it is reasonable to suggest that amongst the many reasons people have given for voting Conservative, a consistent message on the doorstep was that people could not vote for Corbyn. My experience of the doorstep has been that people rejected Corbyn, not necessarily the Labour Party, but rather what they perceived rightly or wrongly Corbyn stood for. The Labour Together project again sourced in the *Guardian* showed Corbyn's popularity quite literally collapsed. [17]

Labour's heartlands, the so called 'red wall', turned their back on the party and held their nose to vote Conservative not out of some new-found loyalty to what the Tories stood for, but because they did not believe Labour was relevant to them anymore.

This was the great betrayal of Labour's values and mission, because the millions of people who need a Labour Government to tackle the social crisis our country faces, among many crises, have been let down by those who assumed control of the Labour Party and failed so miserably in December 2019. These Corbynista's remain trapped in their own interpretation of the world as they want it to be, not the world we face in reality. That is the key lesson of Corbynism, change must have a grounding in reality, people must believe change can happen, in that way Corbynism failed completely.

For a new centre 'left' perspective to be relevant in the 2020s we need to review and understand what key factors in modern society create and sustain inequality. Where does

---

[17] Guardian Graphic. Source YouGov https://www.theguardian.com/politics/2020/jun/18/key-points-from-review-of-2019-labour-election-defeat

climate change fit in this debate and how do we address the needs of the most vulnerable and provide opportunity for the 'Good Society' to flourish? We need a movement on the 'left' to reconnect with its best values such as Crossland's 'Good Society', in order to progress new ideas and transition to a new relevance.

There is a need to listen to and hear the voices of real people not activists and that won't be comfortable for the Labour Party. The new centre 'left' perspective needs to be transformational and truly radical, particularly if it is to address the challenge of climate change, but what does radical mean when we consider the challenge of addressing the realities of modern life? Listening to people and their stories will help Labour reconnect, but the movement and Party has to lead people and shape the debate that comes from that listening. There is a delicate balance to be executed of hearing the voices of people and then answering them not by populism or through focus group policy making but by defining a debate and reshaping the political conversation through clear leadership. Martin Luther King Jr said,

> *"A genuine leader is not a searcher for consensus but a molder of consensus."*[18]

People feel disenfranchised and see politics as an impediment to their lives. They have lost faith in democracy – we often hear the refrain while canvassing that 'they all look the same' or 'they don't do anything for me' and more often than not the non-voters out-number the voters. Goodhart argues how people have come to be divided into two camps:

---

[18] https://www.forbes.com/sites/hennainam/2018/04/04/martin-luther-king-on-leadership-ten-quotes-for-a-changing-world/#537a64bd5c88 accessed on 30th July 2020.

the 'Anywheres', 'who have 'achieved' identities, derived from their careers and education, and 'Somewheres', who get their identity from a sense of place and from the people around them, and who feel a sense of loss due to mass immigration and rapid social change.' [19]

A renewal of Liberal Democracy has to begin with a renewal of the contract between those elected and those electing. We must understand that the threat to the future of Liberal Democracy is real. That is the underlying meaning and lesson of the Brexit referendum result.

Institutional politics was rejected – the European Union, Westminster, the Government, political parties, were all rejected as not relevant to people's lives. The simplistic populist mantra of 'taking back control' was powerful because it tapped into the subconscious fears and paranoia of the population. The lie that thousands of Turks where lining up to invade the country was the worst of far-right dog-whistle politics, but in a vacuum that message resonated which is shameful. Trump, we can argue, talking of the Charlottesville far right protestors as 'very fine people' normalises their behaviour and what they stand for in many people's minds.

The lie about the Turks trades on the demonisation of the other, the simplistic focus on economic nationalism and ethnic superiority. The real tragedy is that Liberal Democratic politicians could not offer a better vision which people could believe in. They were undercut by lies on the side of a big red bus.

Taking back control from what to whom was never the real question. Simply taking back control from whatever people

---

felt had failed them was the reality. People wanted to feel they had power and in defeating the institutions through the referendum regardless of what it truly meant they felt they were giving those same institutions a kicking they believed they deserved. It was as much a rejection of politics as it was anything else. It might be argued that mainstream politicians like Cameron, May, Corbyn and Miliband played directly into the hands of the populists.

We can blame austerity, we can attack the 'Blair' years, but Corbynism was never the answer and Cameron was too busy trying to manage his changing Conservative Party to be bothered at the major crisis his referendum had unleashed.

The centre 'left' and moderate 'right' have therefore squandered a decade, allowing the populists to set up their glib slogan driven tanks on the front lawn of serious politics. The right has been hijacked. The Alt-Right have taken over the Tories driving them further to the extreme and in turn the Corbynistas have driven Labour further to the extreme. The Corbynistas appear less bothered about winning power and using it for social good, they desire, like the populists, to tear the 'system' down – resistance remains the glorious goal. They see the capitalist system as a crucial part of why there are the majority of ills in society. They see bourgeois democracy as compromised and fundamentally undemocratic.

The centre ground, ridiculed by both the populists and Corbynistas, has been abandoned. Painted as institutionalists, as defenders of the status quo, those occupying the centre have failed to offer a vision, and their image has been crafted for them by their opponents.

Fake news, rejecting experts, riling against power at the

'centre', opposing the establishment has become the 'norm' of political discourse. We don't do complex or difficult, we do 'Make America Great Again'.

Coronavirus has however torn through our new border checkpoints and we need a global response. The problem is that a global response is impossible with populist leaders trading on nationalism. For a decade people have rejected globalism and riled against it while capitalism fed off of hate and division to recover from its self-created crash of 2008. A decade of division and nationalism has resulted in a transformed international social landscape, now ripped asunder by the coronavirus.

Protestors take their automatic weapons and storm the state-house in Michigan to protest at the perception their rights are being taken away, egged on by a president who saw them as his constituency. Liberty they see in white supremacy cloaked in a religious justification that their god will protect them from the virus. The West is riddled with examples of the populist far right mobilising resentment to serve the few ultra-capitalists who benefit from the chaos that is created. Capitalism itself has been perverted in this argument. The neoliberalism unleashed in the 1970s and 1980s is devouring the very Liberal Democratic foundations that gave it life.

It is surreal is it not that the likes of Dominic Grieve and Phillip Hammond have common cause with the likes of Alastair Campbell and Tony Blair. The big questions of our time are answered not by serious politicians with serious answers, but glib slogans like 'Get Brexit Done' or 'Stop Brexit'. Even the Liberal Democrats have become a problem in UK politics. Their arrogance and unwillingness to work across the political aisles and their huge mistake of saying that they would simply revoke the referendum result missed the central lesson of that vote. They became as they were in 2015, irrelevant. Sadly, the more Jo Swinson appeared on TV during the 2019 General Election the more damage she did.

So, there is a political undercurrent that has caught each political party in the UK and swept them each into crisis. Indeed, we might argue every Liberal Democracy in the world suffers from the same crisis and malaise. We have faced the coronavirus tragedy with governments in the UK and America whose central problem has been incompetence. That is deeply disturbing and will reinforce peoples spiralling lack of confidence in politicians and in democracy itself.

As we see in countries like Hungary, India or Brazil and also in America, democracy is fragile and coronavirus has exposed the authoritarian tendencies of those who have been in power in those countries. Democracy has made the rise of these authoritarians possible. Accountability and scrutiny are sacrificed in the face of fear of the global virus. We lose our right to vote, our right of movement and free speech. Those most vulnerable are thrust into the forefront as victims of the institutions they work for. The vicious cycle perpetuates the decline of Liberal Democracy in the face of the gravest of threats to our lives.

Western Liberal Democracy faces an existential crisis and that is the fundamental issue the new centre 'left' needs to address. We need to renew what Liberal Democracy means and find the radical 'centre' to directly address the social, environmental and economic problems of our age. Can those who stand up for Liberal Democracy seize the agenda and change the direction of politics, making it relevant to people's real lives again? We need serious politics from serious politicians.

These are, to reiterate, the six strategic areas we will examine which underpin any manifesto of detail that might then emerge.

1. The Rule of Law
2. Democracy and Subsidiarity
3. Universal Rights and Freedoms
4. Equality and Social Justice
5. Opportunity and Economic Security
6. Environmental Sustainability

These are the essential building blocks of Liberal Democracy and the broad arcs of a grand strategy for renewal, that should guide the radicalism needed to answer the challenges of our age. This is not policy and this work offers no detailed manifesto, but rather we set about discussing principles in grand strategy and that is an important distinction. We aim to scope out the principles that could build the framework in which policy might be derived.

Proponents of Liberal Democracy need to establish this new framework before they delve into policy. The direction of overall travel matters if policy is to be coherent and effective. We seek to offer such a structure as a starting point in this debate.

Why a Grand Strategy?

Grand strategy is the overarching political message of a state or mission statement of a state. It is the driving agenda for marshalling the resources of a state and the machinery of a state to achieve a single objective or a set of objectives.

Distinct from strategy, which might be seen as narrowly political or military or economic or social, grand strategy is, instead, the conceptual and organisational overlay from which political, military, economic and social strategies should be derived. Grand strategy could in fact be termed a *gestalt*, in the sense that it is something which is greater than the sum of its parts.

Grand strategy is more than merely the articulation of an objective: it provides the motivation for a state to take a course of action or define an objective to be achieved. A grand strategy should not be a 'pick and mix' of issues that some find relevant and others debate; it should be about the whole.

Grand strategy is more than the single issue. It is about a country's whole perspective on a global level. William Appleman Williams uses the term *Weltanschauung,*

meaning a world view or outlook, the way that a state con-
ceptualises its values and political beliefs in relation to the
world around it. [20]

Political leadership in defining grand strategy is important
if a state is to show purpose and direction. If a renewal of
Liberal Democracy is to be about more than just a list of
polices, then through a grand strategy it can redefine itself
for this generation and beyond.

The importance of grand strategy is that in its absence the
reason behind a state's actions is unclear. The motivation
that drives a state's machinery, such as the military, economy or government is also unclear.

If policies are unclear, or if a state fails to articulate its
grand strategy, then it may be left vulnerable as allies and
adversaries alike find it difficult to understand and interpret
its actions. Without grand strategy, a *Weltanschauung*, the
populists have little to contend with and proponents of
Liberal Democracy have little to offer.

We have explored the failure of mainstream politicians and
that they have ceded ground allowing the political landscape to be shaped by the populists. Liberal Democratic
politicians lack coherence and meaning. They list policies
but lack the overall vision to address the challenges that face
society today. They lack a *Weltanschauung*.

There is nothing wrong with Western Liberal Democratic
ideology, the ideas and principles we will explore are solid

[20] William Appleman Williams, *The Tragedy of American Diplomacy*, W.
W. Norton & Company, New York, fiftieth anniversary edition, 2009,
p. 37 & 38.

foundations. But what do they mean in the modern context? How do they address the challenges we face today? We are not calling for Liberal Democracy to be rewritten as an ideology, far from it. What we are calling for is the renewal of Liberal Democracy in the 21st century based on these building blocks. To use the foundations of Liberal Democracy marshalled in a grand strategy, to give meaning and substance to politicians to then articulate policy that actually means something to people. The point of a grand strategy for Liberal Democracy is that it would offer vision, structure, a *Weltanschauung,* to what at the moment feels like a vacuum in which the populists alone fill the space.

The fulfilment of grand strategy is political, and the tools of the state are used to achieve the goals set out in a state's grand strategy. In our terms for our purpose, the word state can be replaced by Liberal Democracy, and the tools are its ideas. Therefore, when Lieber describes grand strategy as:

> *"The term used to describe how a country will employ the various tools it possesses – military, economic, political, technological, ideological, and cultural – to protect its overall security, values, and national interests."*[21]

This view supports the definition of grand strategy as the *gestalt*. Lieber's reference to the tools of the state that are the technological, military, economic, political and ideological – reflects that grand strategy affects more than just one aspect. Lieber also highlights the importance of grand strategy to national interests and so reinforces the thrust of the argument that a grand strategy defining the renewal of Liberal Democracy in the 2020s would give such substance

---

[21] Robert Lieber, *The American Era*, Cambridge University Press, New York, 2005, p. 40.

to its proponents as to offer a positive alternative to the populists. We seek to use the tools of Liberal Democracy, the six principles we explore, to establish the grand strategy, the framework for renewal, the new *Weltanschauung*.

It is no good just opposing the populists. What is the meaningful substantive vision of the proponents of Liberal Democracy? How do they see the future of society, the economy and the world? What fundamentally are they about in the 21st century?

Liddell Hart's definition of grand strategy in his treatise *Strategy: The Indirect Approach* emphasises the point about policy execution and serves to reinforce that grand strategy sits above policy:

> *"The term 'grand strategy' serves to bring out the sense of 'policy execution'. For the role of grand strategy – higher strategy – is to coordinate and direct all of the resources of a nation, or a band of nations, towards the attainment of the political object of the war – the goal defined by fundamental policy."*[22]

This definition has more in common with how Lieber has defined grand strategy acknowledging its political nature and its relationship to the whole policy of a government. While Hart was writing from a military perspective, in essence proponents of Liberal Democracy are at war with the populists for the future of democracy and as such if they cannot articulate a grand strategic vision of the future they will be condemned to make the same mistakes they have made over the last decade or more. It is as fundamental as

---

[22] Liddell Hart, *Strategy: The Indirect Approach*, Faber and Faber Ltd, London, revised edition 1967, p. 335–336.

that, so understanding why a grand strategy is so important for the future of Liberal Democracy matters.

Then add to this Paul Kennedy's argument that the crux of grand strategy rests in its capacity to coordinate the elements of policy for the preservation and enhancement of the nation's long-term best interests, and again the purpose of a Liberal Democratic grand strategy is reinforced.[23]

Grand strategy must strike a difficult balance: it must be relevant and purposeful in the present but also wise enough to present a forward-looking set of goals that can be followed to shape future policy.

Lieber, Hart and Kennedy all reinforce the theme of coordinating the resources of the state, and the importance of the political aspect in identifying grand strategy. In an article entitled 'Defining and Teaching Grand Strategy' Timothy Andrews Sayle argues:

> *"The definition of grand strategy, however, is elusive, and often operates on a threshold of evidence akin to "I know it when I see it."*[24]

Grand strategy should be readily identifiable, you should know it when you see it. However, grand strategy being publicised and proclaimed isn't enough, it must be understood. It has to be clearly articulated in such a way that it communicates the meaning and reasoning behind policy. It is more than merely the coordination of resources. Taken

---

[23] Paul Kennedy, *Grand Strategies in War and Peace*, Yale University Press, New Haven, 1991, p. 5.

[24] https://www.fpri.org/article/2011/01/defining-and-teaching-grand-strategy/ accessed, 30th July 2020.

together, these writers have each identified a part of grand strategy; the coordination of the tools, the importance of the political aspect, and that it must be clear, publicised and understood.

One of the greatest strengths of the post-Second World war Labour Government was that it had such a *Weltanschauung*. That progressive leap forward was based on more than just a list of policies. It was a vision that people bought into, that was understood, that defined a generation because the politicians had won the hearts and minds of people through the grand strategy of the future Labour proposed and represented.

In our argument for renewing Liberal Democracy as a grand strategy, a new *Weltanschauung*, we set out clearly how the future could and should be saved from the populists. We seek to use the tools of Liberal Democracy to propose a new framework that could win the hearts and minds of people.

The six areas we set out as the framework for renewing Liberal Democracy are connected and linked, they overlap and relate. They are a *gestalt*, strong individually and even stronger when taken together. They offer a new Liberal Democratic Grand Strategy to save our democracy:

1. The Rule of Law
2. Democracy and subsidiarity
3. Universal Rights and Freedoms
4. Equality and Social Justice
5. Opportunity and Economic Security
6. Environmental Sustainability

Magna Carta: The Rule of Law

J C Holt in his seminal work *Magna Carta* said:

> *"The history of Magna Carta is the history not only of a document but also of an argument. The history of the document is a history of repeated re-interpretation. But the history of the argument is a history of a continuous element of political thinking."* [25]

The principle political thought of Magna Carta concerns the rule of law. We make the argument that the principle remains critically relevant today, as much as it was revolutionary in 1215. The 'argument' that Holt describes is that 'all free men' had equality through the rule of law and the application of jurisdiction and justice. [26]

That the charter was written in a time of civil unrest, between a 13th-century king under duress from his barons, should not be lost on our analysis. Holt argues that historians have debated the quality of the Magna Carta and the debate has not been about that alone, but also the origins of the charter and the qualities of the men who produced it. [27]

---

[25] Holt, Magna Carta, third edition 2014, p. 46.
[26] Ibid. Holt. p237.
[27] Ibid. Holt. P232.

The Magna Carta is not some self-conscious statement of emancipation. It is a negotiated deal between factions. It was rewritten in 1216 and also 1225, by many of those same writers of the original document of 1215. It was a document that lasted merely three months before Papal intervention resulted in King John recovering his position, if only for a short time before his death in 1216.

It is also important to distinguish that when the document talks about 'all free men' it does not mean that literally. The writers did not mean women, nor many men, their selection was limited. Our contention in this argument is that 'all free men' should mean everyone; women, men and children were appropriate, i.e. all human beings.

There are a number of key clauses, but in this argument, we contend that Clauses 39, 40, 12 and 61, the order we discuss them, lay fundamental foundations for our modern Liberal Democratic society. We will explore these clauses below.

> Clause 39: *"No free man shall be seized or imprisoned, or stripped of his rights or possessions, or outlawed or exiled, or deprived of his standing in any way, nor will we proceed with force against him, or send others to do so, except by the lawful judgment of his equals or by the law of the land."*[28]

According to Salisbury Cathedral,

> *"This clause established the idea that people could only be judged according to the law, and that even the King himself had to follow the law. King John had previously acted as if the law did not apply to him. The other thing that is important*

---

[28] https://www.salisburycathedral.org.uk/magna-carta-what-magna-carta/key-clauses-magna-carta accessed on 30th July

about this clause is that it stipulates that a person should be judged by a group of their equals (not by the King or his men). The jury system that still exists in Britain today is a continuation of the idea put forward in this clause.[29]

While kings and queens who followed John assumed absolute power and often saw themselves above the law, in the eyes of the wider nation of peoples the rule of law over centuries has gathered power and importance, reinforced by the principle articulated in 1215.

Clause 40: *"To no one will we sell, to no one deny or delay right or justice."*[30]

The law is not for sale, it is not to be bought and sold like a ransom. Justice cannot be withheld or denied in the eyes of the law of the land. This clause can be interpreted in many ways, but today in modern society a debate about access to the law can be defined by monetary access to afford the law and so access to justice is a financial argument. This is perhaps a central grievance of how people have become increasingly disconnected from the institutions designed to protect them. The law today is there only for those who can afford it, yet the law is used to control and subjugate the masses. The inequity of law in modern Liberal Democracies, especially in the US and UK, is a fundamental reason why re-asserting the principles held by Magna Carta matters.

Clause 12 *"No 'scutage' or 'aid' may be levied in our kingdom without its general consent, unless it is for the ransom of our person, to make our eldest son a knight, and (once) to marry our eldest daughter. For these purposes only*

---

[29] Ibid. Salisbury Cathedral.
[30] Ibid. Salisbury Cathedral.

a reasonable 'aid' may be levied. 'Aids' from the city of London are to be treated similarly."[31]

This clause specifies that the king has to seek approval if he desires to raise taxes. It strips the monarch of powers, which is profound, but it also establishes government by consent. The modern debate about executive power is no less controversial. Where should the balance rest between local and national centres of power and in that sense where does power truly reside in the modern global world, such that those governed have any sense of holding that power to account and scrutiny? The likes of Amazon and Apple operate beyond the state and as such beyond the limits of our Liberal Democratic institutions of accountability. A further example of how the unfettered neoliberalism of the last 30 years has centralised capitalist power in corporatism.

Clause 61 *"...We give and grant to the barons the following security: The barons shall elect twenty-five of their number to keep, and cause to be observed with all their might, the peace and liberties granted and confirmed to them by this charter. If we, our chief justice, our officials, or any of our servants offend in any respect against any man, or transgress any of the articles of the peace or of this security, and the offence is made known to four of the said twenty-five barons, they shall come to us – or in our absence from the kingdom to the chief justice – to declare it and claim immediate redress. If we, or in our absence abroad the chief justice, make no redress within forty days, reckoning from the day on which the offence was declared to us or to him, the four barons shall refer the matter to the rest of the twenty-five barons, who may distrain upon and assail us in every way possible, with the support of the whole community of the land, by seizing our castles, lands, possessions, or anything else saving only our own person and those of the queen and our children, until they have secured such redress as they have determined upon."*[32]

This clause sets up a backstop for a congress of the barons to monitor and review the king's actions in honouring the charter. King John particularly hated this clause, amongst the many, for offering up a forum of control which he believed fettered his divine right.

In these clauses you can see the building blocks of our Liberal Democratic system. There are three fundamental points that we might draw from Magna Carta.

Firstly, that the document that was produced in 1215 was for 'all free men'. That was qualified in 1225 with a list of those the re-writers deemed worthy, but the original principle had been in 1215 for a far wider catchment.

Secondly, that the fundamental principle of law beyond the will of the king was established. Law was something established that applied to all and while that might be the 'King's Law' it was also the law of the land and that had a quality to it beyond personal fealty to the monarch.

Thirdly, the Magna Carta has come to mean far more over the centuries, beyond merely the negotiated document of circumstance in 1215. It is a document that draws on a rich history of European charters and treaties where monarchs and church authorities were qualifying their power in the changing social structures of society in medieval Europe.

---

[32] Ibid. Salisbury Cathedral.

In that sense the Magna Carta, like other seminal treaties of their time, represents a waypoint in a deeper debate about the rights of peoples. If the Magna Carta was just a document for the barons and king that presided over its creation then the consequences of it have been far reaching way beyond their intention.

Magna Carta sets down in English terms, in 1215, despite its later qualification, that it was written for 'all free men'. It contains an embodiment of the principle of the rule of law. This is crucial to our argument because we contend that it is a foundation and an origin of modern Liberal Democracy. It was not the only one, but crucially one of the most important. It would be a stretch to argue that Magna Carta was the first Liberal Democratic treatise, it was no such thing, for one it was for all 'free men' and did not seek to be universal in its application of rights. But, as Holt argues it was more than a document, it was a political idea. That idea was the rule of law. The rule of law is critical because it is beyond and above the government of the day. The pedestal that Magna Carta has been put on, rightly or wrongly – which is a debate for historians – is that the king or the state authority is not above the law, but the securer of the law in the interests of 'all free men'.

The perverse position of Trump or Johnson in the modern context is that they have governed from a point of view, we might suggest, where it appears they consider the law is there to serve them. The elected authoritarianism they appear to embody runs back it could be argued to the 'divine right' expressed by King John and the very reason the barons drew up Magna Carta. That is a fundamental battle of our age not just theirs. It is a battle to reassert the values espoused by the Magna Carta. That the law is there for 'all free men'. The quality of that is in how the rule of law has over centuries following Magna Carta become universal. Time and again commentators and politicians speak of Magna Carta in that context, that no one least of all the president or prime minister is above the law.

So, to paraphrase Natasha Henry, when the Slavery Abolition Act was passed in 1833, an act of Parliament that officially abolished slavery in most British colonies, freeing more than 800,000 enslaved Africans in the Caribbean and South Africa as well as a small number in Canada. It received Royal Assent on August 28, 1833, and took effect on August 1, 1834. [33]

It became the law of the land and all territories that it applied to around the globe. The key point being that the law was universal and extended English law to 'all free men.' It is why the United States Emancipation Proclamation and law of 1863 is so fundamental and was fought over so bitterly. The rule of law in Liberal Democracy is fundamental.

If we add to this argument the clauses that discuss the assembly of Barons and the King's need to request approval when raising taxes then the basic principles of government by consent begin to emerge. The principles of representative governance however weak are established. We begin to separate and codify power which undermines the divine right of the king. Magna Carta in this sense is fundamental to our modern Liberal Democratic society. While the debate over the centralisation of power in both the UK and US is a topic in its own right, the point about the separation of powers and government by consent is crucial to our argument.

---

[33] https://www.britannica.com/topic/Slavery-Abolition-Act accessed on 30th July 2020.

The first 'pillar' of renewal is to restore faith and trust in the 'rule of law' for 'all free men'. The underlying principle of modern society looking forward must be that access to the law is not contingent on someone's ability to pay or the colour of their skin, their gender or sexuality. It should not be the case that the quality of justice is determined by the amount of it you can buy. This should not be a charter for litigation, but we must not be afraid of access to the law 'for all free men'. Equal access to the law must mean that for those that cannot afford the law that should not be an impediment to justice. People feel institutions are beyond them and out of reach, redressing that point in one of the most fundamental areas of life, i.e. law and order, matters. The law must be equal, it must be applied fairly and independently, it must be 'for all free men' regardless of status or position, it must be universal and without qualification. Scrutiny and inquiry must be independent and just. The old adage of being seen to be just applies in this analysis. It should be established that the judiciaries place in modern society is reaffirmed by its connection to people not it's self-service as an institution relevant only to those that can afford it.

That's why it is so important, because the judiciary has to be the guardian of the 'rule of law', empowered and unfettered. The role of the Attorney General linking the political to the judicial is crucial and the way that the role has been politicised in recent times both through the Iraq War of 2003 and in Brexit undermines the integrity of that position. The officers of state that represent the 'law' must retain that degree of separation that defines the quality of their action. The 'bending' of law to suit the political will of those in power must be challenged and the separation of power and scrutiny enforced through means that enjoy confidence in the wider country. Those who guard and apply the law do so for us all and it must be seen as such. That is why this 'pillar' of our renewed Liberal Democracy is so fundamental.

A Revolution of Democracy

"We the People of the United States, in Order to form a more perfect Union, establish Justice, insure domestic Tranquillity, provide for the common defence, promote the general Welfare, and secure the Blessings of Liberty to ourselves and our Posterity, do ordain and establish this Constitution for the United States of America."[34]

From Magna Carta's medieval origins evolved the revolutionary ideas of the 17th and 18th Centuries. The American Constitution and Bill of Rights did not simply appear on tablets of stone handed down from on high. The years of evolution in political thought in Europe and the colonies led to a bedrock of philosophical and political radicalism that in many ways defines not simply the birth of the United States, but also the French Revolution and the continuing evolution of parliamentary democracy in England. From Thomas Paine to John Locke, the great liberal thinkers of the age pondered the deeper appreciation of the rights of 'man'. While politicians like Maddison and Hamilton created documents to reflect those same principles.

---

[34] https://constitutionus.com/#constitution accessed on 30th July 2020.

We must acknowledge the role played by the Levellers and radicals in Cromwell's Parliamentary Army, even if they were only on the edges of the English Revolution, and of the religious few who took their puritanism to the new world and developed new forms of local government. Democracy as we know it was born of conflict, suppression and subversion. We should not forget also, the utter colonialist suppression of the lands they invaded. Think about the indigenous, black and white blood that was spilled developing 'new forms of local government' on native lands. The suppression, theft and genocide committed by the same founding fathers should be acknowledged and addressed as a stain on our history.

Indeed, we should acknowledge that the indigenous nations had constitutional arrangements that understood the values espoused by the founding fathers long before the American Revolution. Chief Oren Lyons, an Onondaga and an associate professor of American studies at the State University at Buffalo, said in a 1987 article in the New York Times that: "

> *Before Europeans settled upstate in the 1600's, the Five Nations of the Iroquois lived under a constitution that had three main principles, peace, equity or justice and 'the power of the good minds.'"*[35]

The late 18th century was a time of tumult and conflict, but also an awakening of nascent liberalism, gathered from many sources and influences. The condition of 'man' was central to thinkers like Thomas Paine and John Locke. The ideas of liberty, economic and political freedoms underpinned their

---

[35] https://www.nytimes.com/1987/06/28/us/iroquois-constitution-a-forerunner-to-colonists-democratic-principles.html accessed on 30th July 2020.

treatises and documents. Of importance in this debate is the context in which those freedoms were debated in the 18th century. Slavery was still lawful, the rights of all 'men' were not equal.

Many of those early liberal thinkers only spoke of 'white men' and in that context the founding fathers of the American Revolution were not fighting for freedom for all, but only in a qualified sense for white freedom. Within that they also did not see universal suffrage as something that pertained to all 'white men', the wider population was deemed too much a 'mob'. Like with Magna Carta the original documents of the Revolution were deficient not necessarily in words but in how they were enacted. They nonetheless established a direction of travel. Even today the battle for equality in the true sense that we might interpret the American Constitution in the 21st century, that every-one has unalienable rights', is one that runs through the heart of American politics.

The aims and objectives set out in the 17th and 18th century by the founding fathers of the United States are very rele-vant today in the continued fight for universal equality. That must be a thread of principle that runs through the heart of any Liberal Democratic renewal. The words must mean what they say, and we must live by them in our institutions and in policy. If we embrace the American Constitution, Bill of Rights and the many documents that define the rev-olution in democracy, they are not an end in-of-themselves held in aspic, they are living documents and principles that need constant renewal.

The choice is also between building on the established documents or recrafting them in a modern setting. In terms of the American Constitution and Bill of Rights they have consistently been amended. There is an inherent tension here, can the documents reflect the values we seek to renew and recast, or are they so anachronistic they lack the flexibility to achieve the goal we are arguing for? This is an important question that deserves deeper forensic analysis. In this work let's at least argue a baseline for such analysis. Our prescription for renewal is based on the ideas they embodied, more than the documents themselves.

In his *Second Treatise of Government* published in 1689, [36] John Locke outlined his views on the origins and structure of legitimate, constitutionally elected government, and developed his ideas of social contract theory which referenced themes about the exercise of power. Spencer Guier argues:

> *"One obvious influence would be the ideas related to natural rights found in the Constitution and the Declaration of Independence. The Declaration of Independence (US 1776) states, "that all men are created equal, that they are endowed by their Creator with certain unalienable Rights, that among these are Life, Liberty and the pursuit of Happiness." In Chapter II of Second Treatise, Locke argues for "a state also of equality wherein all the power and jurisdiction is reciprocal, no having more than another." He then goes on to state, "no one ought to harm another in his life liberty or possessions." Locke's influence extends beyond the specific vocabulary of life, liberty, and the pursuit of happiness planted in the Declaration of Independence, but also extends to the idea that it is the responsibility of the state to ensure the protection and preservation of these*

---

[36] John Locke, Second Treatise of Government, Watchmaker Publishing, 31 Mar. 2011.

natural rights as implied throughout both the Constitution and Declaration of Independence."[37]

At the heart of the debate is the affirmation of democracy resting with the people, not in the government itself. In essence democracy of, by and for the people meant exactly that and it was the state's, both federal and local, role to defend those 'natural' rights. The parallel to our modern condition is that the American colonies felt remote from the old world and as such new ideas, not least written forms of agreement and charter were common place. The remoteness also developed a sense of exclusion and misunderstanding between the peoples of the colonies and the king. There was a sense of division which drove a wedge between England and her overseas American territories. Not just physically but also philosophically. The sense of injustice seething with ferment in matters of taxation and decision could easily be transposed to today and the debates about Europe or indeed the role of central government in the UK.

We have become accustomed to being governed and giving our consent. We acquiesce and take a minimal part in the business of governance. We look to be led and when the quality of that leadership is lacking it exposes the frailties of the system designed to empower the representatives and executive who govern in our name. We might say that Brexit has exposed such frailties.

The Western Liberal Democratic traditions of government and civil bureaucracy have been developed over the last two centuries to the point that the body of government is itself a beast, a monolith, that perpetuates itself. It justifies itself

---

[37] http://guierlaw.com/john-lockes-influence-on-the-united-states-constitution/ accessed on 30th July 2020.

and its power by virtue of its being. The disconnection from people and their lives is found in the centralisation of that power. In the UK especially, there are different pressures pulling the state apart and at the same time focusing power at the centre. The emergence of regional mayors and of devolved assemblies has augmented local government, but power and financial control are retained largely at the centre of Whitehall in London. These so-called devolved bodies are tinkering around the edges of the fundamental seat of power sited in Whitehall.

Subsidiarity is a forgotten principle that most governments preach when in opposition and misplace when in power. The ideas of localism are only as good as a government willing to let its power go and allow variation and dissent.

Our vote matters only when it counts and in modern UK politics some votes matter more than others in a first past the post electoral system that sees those seeking power fight over an increasingly narrow selection of society. Disconnection is real when you feel your vote and voice do not matter. The populists exploit these tensions and we witnessed this in the Brexit referendum.

As governments have been challenged by populists they have invariably withdrawn into themselves and become further divorced from people. They have become reclusive elites and that compounds the anger and frustration people feel towards them.

The second 'pillar' of renewal is the new contract required between the elected and electors. We need to reinvigorate the democracy we have with a fresh perspective on participation and a willingness to challenge the institutional arrangements which govern over us. Reflecting on the base principles espoused in the American Declaration of Independence and in the Bill of Rights, can we rediscover the radicalism in free speech alongside tolerance and human rights in the age of social media? Can we protect participatory democracy from vested interests? Can we define a new relationship between people and government?

The rejection of the European Union in Brexit was based in part on the idea it was an elite that governed over people without consent. It was not a Europe of peoples, but rather a Europe of institutions remote from its peoples. In driving for greater unity, the European Union has exposed the diversity and inequality in the condition of peoples around the continent. The North–South divide is a major fault line in Europe, as much as East–West. Division is sown still by national interest where those considered at the heart of Europe (Germany, France and the Benelux nations) dictate terms to those others such as Greece, Spain and Hungary.

This is not a Europe of equals. It is not a United Kingdom of equals either. In establishing a new contract, we have to think about how our democracy works, how representative government can be inclusive and break the argument that 'politics doesn't apply to me'. We break the populists through the application of our Liberal Democratic values espoused so eloquently in the American Declaration of Independence looking forward defining a new contract to change our democracy and steer it away from the precipice we found ourselves on through Brexit.

We need a modern democratic revolution. If the concern is the rise of China and India and in their ascendance, they undermine the 'West's' political and economic position, we should answer the questions posed by the rise of these other centres of power by having confidence in our democratic values which involve people in government in a more inclusive way. We should avoid great power rivalry and nationalism at all costs, given the history of were that conflict leads humanity. A renewal of Liberal Democracy should embed the global interests of peace and economic prosperity as positive ideals. If people have a vested interest in democracy that ownership will bring with it security. Through transforming our voting system, truly devolving power, embracing subsidiarity properly and empowering localism away from the centre, through empowering government by the people and for the people we can offer an opportunity to reinvigorate Liberal Democracy. That is much more powerful than any populist siren voice.

In the late Victorian era, great civic edifices, like Manchester City Hall, were built that reflected the power of the age divested in places like Manchester. London was powerful, but it was not the only centre of power. Now London eclipses the rest of the country and as such the dichotomy between the capital and the country is stark. Division is worse in places like Boston or Clacton because democracy means little to people when it is remote to them and meaningless. If a vote had value in changing the condition of people it would transform people's value in it. Localism is not about simply devolving power, although to begin with that would be a solid start, it is also about the quality of local leadership to take up that power and be effective. We have seen such a hollowing out of local government over decades that this cultural shift we are speaking of here will require time and faith because things will not transform over-night and mistakes will be made.

As Churchill suggested democracy is not perfect, but neither is 'man'. We are imperfect and as such our aptitude in the exercise of power will take time to re-establish at local levels. Central government has to act as the insurer of failure and underwrite the devolution of power. While national standards might be set, the local interpretation of those standards needs to find form that empowers people. Local models of mutualism, cooperative relationships between geographic and institutional places that builds competence but also aligns services to natural scales is what we need.

One size fits all electoral boundaries only serve to draw lines on maps, but genuine coalitions of interest and need can better reflect local priorities. Unitary local government empowers communities by securing direct lines of accountability. The English County system reinforces the disconnect people feel not only because it is literally physically remote in most cases but it also lacks local accountability. Delivering the big services like social care and education need not conform to rigid boundaries but reflect cooperative relationships in regions that deliver effectiveness and accountability. Geographies that reflect this natural alignment can be powerful. Local can be a myriad of these delivery mechanisms overlaid with democratic accountability and scrutiny worthy of the name.

The centre must give up power and devolve this to local government. The danger is that the centre determines the shape of local government. The evolution of local democracy has to come from the ground up. It has to be functional, it needs to be accountable and it has to deliver results that make a difference to people's lives. While the centre might establish principles such as a proportional voting system, or codes of conduct, the essential point of subsidiarity needs to be unleashed. Greater Manchester is not rural Lincolnshire, and therefore devolution of democracy has to reflect natural communities.

We can be inventive and should encourage innovation while holding local government to account for the services they deliver. So much of the Brexit referendum was focused on the disenfranchisement people felt towards a system they had no perceived stake in. Government of the people, by the people and for the people must mean exactly what it says in order to renew our Liberal Democracy.

If we only think of democracy in traditional terms, however, we miss the new relationships people have with information technology and the way society is itself changing through technology. We said earlier that capitalism serves itself, that people have found themselves slaves to the capital system, rather than the capital system being there to serve people. Democratising capitalism is revolutionary, but it is also vital if Liberal Democracy is to find relevance in this brave new world.

In this sense, we are not simply talking about democratising the boardroom. That the modern executive boards of major companies remain a white middle-aged male preserve is a truism. That the bedrock of our economy in business and entrepreneurial talent is founded in small enterprises is also true. The economy as we see it in our daily lives is small, human and representative. The 'deeper' economy that we do not see in markets, national and supranational companies, is another world. States have trouble relating to this kind capitalism. This is the elite world of investors, pension funds and stock markets. They define our prosperity and make or break our economic world. Thus, their power is global and also very personal. Your mortgage, your business, your job depends on the health of this 'deeper' capitalist world. So what role does democracy have to play, where is the accountability and social responsibility here? The idea of democratising capitalism needs to reflect more than revolutionary ideals that really mean nothing in reality. What is needed here is a mature relationship of power and scrutiny reflecting a symbiosis – capitalism needs people and people need capitalism.

Do we have the mechanisms to understand the meaning of globalism? Do we have the mechanisms to allow people to shape capitalism? This is not a question for governments alone. The information age reaches inside people's homes, it's 24-hour news media, it's smart phones and technology that connects the world beyond governments and the state.

Facebook, Amazon and Apple are all supranational businesses that are beyond the state. They turnover more money in a year than many small nations. They are subject to the law only where the law can be made to apply to them. The recent battles over tax in Europe has exposed how these corporate organisations are new powerbrokers on the international stage. They have power like states and can bully states. Facebook for example has the power to directly influence elections. They wield democratic power to shape governments. The populists have already learnt how to manipulate this world. They have enlisted Facebook and Twitter to be the disseminators of hate and division. They use Facebook and Twitter to subvert democracy, allied with Russia and China. These are dangerous times for the truth. Facts get in the way and the populists through data and targeting know how to use this new world to get directly into the homes of billions of people. That is why Liberal

Democracy has to address the issue of how to bring the likes of Facebook and Twitter out of the shadows and into the light.

Turning this on its head, this is a question of how Liberal Democracy creates a system of scrutiny and accountability in a global setting to regulate and moderate the power of these corporate entities. Democratising capitalism is a major theme of any democratic renewal. We want the benefits of Amazon or Twitter, but they cannot be allowed to dictate the terms of the game by themselves. We want them to be a part of the relationship developed to express democratic renewal. That means participation and inclusion, openness and transparency.

Democracy is fragile. Populists know this. They understand how to bend the rules, twist the reality to suit their agenda. It's not as if this is solely the preserve of the right. On the left the keyboard warriors are as virulent. While mainstream politicians appear on the six o'clock news, they've already been undercut by the information revolution online. Proponents of Liberal Democracy have to understand the nature of the new playing field. While mainstream politicians play normal 2D chess, the populists are playing 3D chess.

Proponents of Liberal Democracy really need to get a grip of this brave new world in a way they haven't yet. They need to beat the populists at their own game, be better at it and hold to their values of transparency and openness.

When we talk about the American Constitution or the Bill of Rights and the radicalism contained within these documents, the ideas they espoused. It's how we apply those ideals to the battle we have just described that will determine the strength of future democracy. When we say 'we the people', 'by the people, for the people' that ideal has as much power today as it did 245 years ago. We need to define what it means by better understanding how we bring democracy to the modern world and back into people's lives.

Universal Human Rights

"In the centre of our movement stands the idea of a Charter of Human Rights, guarded by freedom and sustained by law."[38]

When the European Convention on Human Rights was established in 1948 at the Congress of Europe, in the aftermath of the Holocaust and the atrocities of the Second World War, its relevance and need, was it could be argued, manifest. Manifest not just in regard to the principles it espoused in the post war period but also in the number of nations that signed up to the Convention. It was finalised in 1953 and the United Kingdom was the first nation to ratify the Charter. The idea of universal rights underwritten by a court of justice in the Hague was profound, we might say it was akin to Magna Carta writ large on the European scale.

The Council of Europe today consists of 47 nations, now including Montenegro. All 47 are signatories of the ECHR.

For more than 68 years the ECHR has underwritten individual human rights in Europe. The imperfect relationship

---

[38] http://www.churchill-society-london.org.uk/WSCHague.html accessed on 30th July 2020.

between states and this supranational body has become increasingly strained and tense. That tension being between domestic laws of nation states and the decisions from the court of the ECHR which have become points of contention for example in the Brexit debate. Member states of the European Union are obliged to become signatories of the ECHR.

In the fervour of anti-European sentiment expressed by Brexiteers they cite the ECHR as the next big battle they propose to fight having as they see it 'won' Brexit. The *FT* cites Dominic Cummings:

> *"In a blog post from March 2018, before he entered government, Mr Cummings said: 'We're leaving the EU next March. Then we'll be coming for the ECHR referendum and we'll win that by more than 52-48…"*[39]

Dismantling the ECHR is a goal, alongside the withdrawal from other international obligations and treaties, proposed by the Brexiteers like Dominic Cummings. Their obsession with Europe is feverish and they perceive that the ECHR has overridden domestic law and interfered with the rights of nations to determine their own laws.

The third pillar of renewal for Liberal Democracy is to assert the universal importance of human rights and how organisations like the ECHR need reform in the 21st century to meet the challenges of today. It would be a mistake to simply defend the status quo. That institutional indifference would hand the initiative to the likes of Cummings. The battle must go beyond the institutions and to the people

---

[39] Data case defeat increases Tory pressure to quite ECHR, Financial Times, Feb 13, 2020.

themselves. It is they that matter most in this debate. Proponents of Liberal Democracy must win the hearts and minds of people on the key subject of their human rights and how we protect them.

Again, Magna Carta has lessons for this debate. If we say that the 'rule of law' is beyond the government, as Magna Carta suggested it was beyond the king, it is for 'all free men'. Then the protection of that law beyond the government is crucial. Combined with the 'natural' rights of 'man' enshrined in law in part through the 1998 Human Rights Act, then the defender of such rights is not simply the state, it must be something greater. Laws change, but do rights? Are rights unalienable and given for all time? Are they universal not just in reach but in being? Of course, these debates stretch back in history as fundamental philosophical and political paradigms.

If we accept the need for universal human rights the debate could reset itself, back to the same conversation that was had in 1948 at the Congress of Europe. Why have the ECHR in the first place?

We need this debate today, not in some romanticised review of the post-Second World War period, but using the principles established in 1948 in the modern context. Why is the ECHR relevant in the 21st century?

We should also acknowledge that those arguing for withdrawal from the ECHR are not arguing against human rights. Crudely, they argue that sovereign nations should determine their laws without interference from supranational bodies. Again, the rationale of the ECHR needs asserting to counter this populist view. Very simply if we accept that human rights are universal, that they are unalienable and natural, then they apply beyond the state, therefore they are best protected by as universal or as global a commitment as can be possible.

The tension here is between those that would suggest national sovereignty trumps universal human rights. The debate seems almost oxymoronic. Why would anyone in a democracy seek to deny universal human rights that reinforce liberties we see individuals enjoying unless through the exercise of that sovereignty they sought to interfere with those same universal human rights. It is often suggested in debate with Brexiteers that they believe in the primacy of self-control and sovereignty; and that a supranational body such as the ECHR actually denies the right of nations to determine their own set of rights for their populations. That sense of self determination is fundamental to their understanding of subsidiarity.

Thus, the question becomes one of who can remove someone else's rights. If a majority of the population vote to remove the right of free speech enshrined in international law through the ECHR then can they do that? As signatories to the ECHR those individual freedoms are given a backstop through the court at the Hague. Should the majority by right of sovereignty have the power to rule over the minority when it comes to basic human rights? These are fundamental questions that challenge our appreciation of what globalism and internationalism mean in the 21st century.

Proponents of Liberal Democracy need to understand that in promoting universal human rights they are not promoting institutions or treaties. The battle is for people's understanding that their right to protest, to free speech and expression, or to religion, to vote, and all of the other rights enshrined in the ECHR are their rights. They are rights owned by no one else and nor should they be – this is why the foundations of human rights, first laid into law in the Magna Carta, matter so much.

They enjoy these rights as individuals because of the ECHR not in spite of it. In this sense the argument is one of values and principles that undercut the narrow nationalistic language of the Brexiteers. The question for the Brexiteers is in their model of sovereignty, who will determine what rights are given and how will they be secured under a system defined purely by national sovereignty? If the only guarantee of rights is through the state, then who controls the state controls those rights, which fundamentally undermines the principles of Magna Carta. Human rights are not laws, they are beyond law if we see them as universal and natural, but they should be protected by the law such that no one in authority in a position of control within a state can snuff them out.

The danger with the populists is that their authoritarian tendencies drift towards undermining rights in favour of order and suppression. They seek popular consent via a 'vox pops' kind of reality politics, whereby the masses as they perceive them are freed from the yoke of liberal institutionalism. They claim they seek to 'drain the swamp', when in fact they wind up controlling the swamp for their own agenda. In that sense the backstop of the ECHR is a vital tool in maintaining our human rights in the face of the populists or whoever is in government.

Therefore, this third pillar of renewal underwrites all of the rest, as it lays the bedrock of freedoms we enjoy and should lead to protections that ensure universalism and our natural rights.

Equality and Social Justice

The deep-rooted philosophical principles of democracy, human rights and the rule of law go back centuries, deeply engrained in Liberal thinking. We might suggest that the battle over inequality and social injustice are a relatively modern addition to traditional Liberal Democracy. Liberals paved the way for Socialists and in a Western context the relationship between Social Democracy/Democratic Socialism and Liberal Democracy is important. The Liberal Party in British politics displaced by Labour during the 20th century has always had a tense relationship with Democratic Socialism. Accusing the proponents of it in the Labour Party of stealing their social liberal 'clothes'. Whether we look to Hobhouse, Hobson or Keynes, the social liberalism they espoused underpins modern centre left thinking. In the face of populism such churlish divisions on the left misunderstand the rich traditions of Liberalism and Democratic Socialism that define the context that underpins our case for a renewal of Liberal Democracy.

The success of Liberal Democracy should concern Democratic Socialists and Liberals alike, and their shared experience over the last one hundred years is of more time than not spent under Conservative Governments because among many reasons, the centre and left were divided.

The fourth pillar of renewal for Liberal Democracy is a rediscovery of this relationship between the battle for social justice and the values and principles of Liberal Democracy. We go so far in this argument as to suggest that the centre ground of British and American politics is this coalition of Liberal and Social Democratic traditions and unless they find a consensus moving forward the battle will continue to be lost to the populists. That would be a self-serving selfish reality that they bring upon themselves if the traditions are too arrogant to realise they have more in common than divides them.

Poverty and social injustice are as Beveridge, a Liberal, identified in his Parliamentary Report, stains on any Liberal Democracy. Government of the people, by the people and for the people must lift the condition of society well beyond poverty and deliver social justice. The ills of society as Beveridge identified them are as relevant today as in 1940s.

This pillar of renewal underpins the inclusiveness needed to reach out to the disenfranchised who say so often on the doorstep that politics means nothing to them because it does nothing for them.

To be clear Democratic Socialism is not Socialism in a purest sense and therein lies the divide at the heart of the Labour Party. Socialists want to overthrow the state in a revolution of change that transforms society. Democratic Socialism, like Social Liberalism, seeks to use the state to reform and evolve society. In this argument the renewal of Liberal Democracy can be radical but it is not a revolution in waiting. As we saw with the 2019 General Election, such revolutions are not connected to reality and do not enjoy wide support, rather the populists are able to draw strength from opponents like Corbyn because they have thoroughly misunderstood society. Every time the 'hard' left take control of the Labour Party and present themselves as the alternative, society reject them because they are divorced from society. The strength of Asquith, Atlee, Wilson and Blair was the moment in history in which they united society in a progressive leap of faith. Is it not about time the centre left of British Politics learnt from its own history?

In the 21st century it is a scandal that in modern Britain child poverty or food poverty exists on the scale it does. It is a simple injustice that people do not have enough money to maintain a home, to put food on the table, to pay basic bills and sustain their households. The deprivation we see in society is a fundamental social evil that any renewal of Liberal Democracy must set itself against. Deprivation in education, work, health and wellbeing are all social injustices that undermine Liberal Democracy.

Emma MacLennan sat on the Social Justice Commission established by John Smith, the former Leader of the Labour Party in 1992. In an article commemorating the 25th anniversary of the Commission she wrote:

> *"The Commission on Social Justice established by John Smith set out four propositions of enormous importance to its founder: that the welfare state should be a 'springboard for economic opportunity'; that education and training are vital and need investment; that there must be a balance between employment, education and family responsibilities to give people better life choices; and that local government and public services play a key role in a just society."*[40]

---

[40] https://cpag.org.uk/welfare-rights/resources/article/25-years-reflections-social-justice accessed 30th July 2020.

John Smith himself said:

> *"It is a sense of revulsion at injustice and poverty and denied opportunity, whether at home or abroad, which impels people to work for a better world… Instead of carrying the miserable burden of mass unemployment, we could be investing in new technology and new skills, training and retraining our talented people to face a fiercely competitive world; instead of our education system declining and our health service fracturing, we could be building high-quality public services which extend security and opportunity to every family in the land; instead of a society diminished by the violence and dishonesty of crime, we could be building strong communities which provided opportunity as well as protection for every citizen. There is so much we can do; there is so much we need to do."*[41]

As a pillar of renewal for Liberal Democracy we need to heed the lessons of the 1992–94 Social Justice Commission and establish today a new commission with the express mission of renewing the debate and examination of poverty and social injustice in the 2020s. The principles and focus of the 1992 Commission are a solid starting point for a fresh and deep examination of these key social issues.

Populists have been able to tap into the sense of anger and deep frustration people feel when jobs and businesses are perceived to ebb and flow on the whims of global markets. They play the nationalist card to embolden a sense of injustice. The arguments over immigration and foreign investors all roll into a narrative of blaming the 'other'. These base prejudices are fuelled by poverty and exclusion. Institutions

---

[41] https://cpag.org.uk/welfare-rights/resources/article/25-years-reflections-social-justice accessed on 30th July 2020.

are remote and do not meet the needs of people. The police, the government at all levels, education and social care are all edifices of the state that stand juxtaposed to the experiences and life chances of so many. It is this disconnection that the populists prey on.

The Labour Party is struggling to understand why it has lost support of the northern 'red wall' and it consistently misses the point. It is not about Brexit, that is an expression of the deeper problem. It is not about a metropolitan elite running the party, that is an expression of the disconnection. It is not about policies of nationalisation or about factions like Momentum, they are distractions. It is about the need for the Labour Party to connect with people's lives.

As we quoted earlier, Martin Luther King Jr said: "A genuine leader is not a searcher for consensus but a molder of consensus." To be accurate we should acknowledge Luther King's anti-capitalist views which underpin his words. In order to lead Labour has to listen and then mould consensus. It has to do that from a position of understanding. Indeed, the whole centre and left of politics needs to craft a new consensus to sustain any renewal of Liberal Democracy.

Now is the time, more than ever, to think about how to bring the left back in from the cold. This will require more concrete change and framing the national discussion with constant reference to solidarity, this is the only way proponents of Liberal Democracy will appeal to the aspirations of all of the young people who put their confidence in Corbyn. There must be room in the broad church for them. Yet again, we draw a distinction between the supporters of ideals and Corbyn's inner circle. The soft centre right of British politics is equally important because within a new consensus and broad church the leap of faith we are arguing for here could be cemented for the next generation.

John Smith knew this in 1992, following Labour's fourth election defeat in a row. In 2020 Labour has lost four elections in a row and been out of power for a decade. The Labour Party does not have a right to represent the centre left if they do not understand what that means. If the Labour Party is not the vehicle, nor the Liberal Democrats, then the centre left needs to admit this and look to something new. The selfishness of politicians is that 'turkeys do not vote for Christmas' and tribalism is a great barrier to change. The populists have the centre left and moderate right exactly where they want them and the critical point is that only those on the centre left and moderate right can break that hold.

The crisis of Liberal Democracy is also a social crisis. That social crisis needs to be properly understood so that the renewal of Liberal Democracy that is offered is genuine and one that people recognise reflects their lives and answers their need for hope.

President Obama impressed this argument about hope. While the analysis of the problems and the causes of social injustice are critical to finding solutions, the solutions need to be clearly articulated and believable. Change will only happen if people believe it is possible. Hope therefore is crucial. It's the ingredient of Liberal Democracy that populists ridicule but also fear. That hard-line Conservatives paint as fantasy, but when harnessed properly is a force of nature that has a history of moments of profound change. 1906, 1945, 1966, 1997 are progressive milestones in modern history because they unleashed hope. Hope grounded in policy that was well thought out and rooted in people's lives.

This is why this pillar of renewing Liberal Democracy matters, it connects the mission, the aims of renewal with people. It shows not just empathy and solidarity, but substance and meaning. In understanding social injustice and seeking policy to directly address poverty and exclusion, the proponents of Liberal Democracy harness a very powerful political tool, hope, and it is this arguments' contention that hope trumps fear, literally.

Opportunity and Economic Security

The challenges posed by globalisation alongside the inequities created by corporatism and neoliberal capitalism have led over the last decade to a seething mass of anger amongst populations in the West because jobs, prosperity and investment are shifting to the East. There is a strong undercurrent of division and disconnected antagonism in communities across the West. From small towns that feel cut off from the economic prosperity of metropolises to urban pockets of deep deprivation, the economic challenges facing the West are significant.

Child poverty and food bank use was increasing well before covid limited economic opportunity and created the greatest economic downturn in recorded history. The divisions within society are greater because of the dichotomy experienced by communities living next door to each other. In some cases, for example, life expectancy in a poorer community is ten years less than the more affluent community literally across the road.

Charles Booth's maps of poverty in 19th century London offer a profound graphical depiction of poverty alongside affluence in the capital. [42]

---

[42] https://booth.lse.ac.uk/map/16/-0.1175/51.4886/100/0)

Booth's maps depicts poverty, or as he described the social classes as ranging from – "lowest class. Vicious, semi-criminal." To the affluent – "Middle class. Well-to-do." These are very Victorian descriptions and reflect prejudices about class that are deep-seated. His maps offer a stark picture of people in poverty living alongside people with affluence which is a very important part of our analysis. [43]

In the modern era using multiple points of quantitative analysis from child poverty to income deprivation the Ministry of Communities, Housing and Local Government Deprivation Indices depict the same stark realities across the country in 2019. Their online tool allows you to see the quantification of poverty on multiple levels and you can drill down to your own community and see the comparisons of data. [44]

These two examples are graphical in the way they show through maps and colour the nature of division within society. They are insightful in that they offer a window through which we see poverty and affluence interwoven in our communities.

There is a fundamental point expressed here about the impact of western capitalism. Governments have failed to lift people consistently out of poverty.

The gentrification of London, Manchester and Leeds, just three metropolitan examples, is leading many people to be pushed out into smaller peripheral communities who have

---

[43] https://booth.lse.ac.uk/map/16/-0.1175/51.4886/100/0)
Base map © OpenStreetMap contributors - accessed 30th July 2020.
[44] http://dclgapps.communities.gov.uk/imd/iod_index.html accessed 30th July 2020.

neither the infrastructure or means to cope and this has increased tensions and divisions. Again, Luce's argument of displacement reflects this stark social disconnection as we have referenced.

There is an important story to be told of people disconnected from social mobility and the undercurrent of poverty pervading many communities in the 'West'. The populists have preyed on this disconnection selling a story of economic nationalism and blaming globalism and liberal institutions for the economic ills of society. That's where the 'take back control' or 'Make America Great Again' messages resonate. It is the anger channelled through the Brexit referendum or 2016 Presidential election that shows how serious these undercurrents have become.

Any renewal of Liberal Democracy must directly address the economic inequities we see manifest in society not simply as a result of covid, but which have been systemic for over a decade or more. Western capitalism has eaten itself alive perpetuating the economic decline and narrowing global wealth into the hands of an absolute few. This is not a point of envy, it is statement of fact. Therefore, the question is not one of how that wealth can be redistributed, the battle with those elites to achieve redistribution alone will not fix the problems people face in their daily lives. It may be morally unjust that wealth is so concentrated, but it's changing the economic system itself that can offer redress to those in poverty.

Any renewal of Liberal Democracy needs to focus on policies that lift people directly out of poverty. It's an economic realignment that is required and selling that priority to people is about more than divisions over nationalisation or tax and spend. There is a more fundamental question that needs addressing which is how is the economy structured – Infrastructure, skills and education, science and research, and new business creation are all major policy areas any government should be focusing on. Proponents of Liberal Democracy need to win the hearts and minds of people through a vision of a meaningful economic future.

When Labour came into Government in 1997 there was an acknowledgement that investment in its heartlands, the former industrial areas of the country, was long overdue. The preceding two decades of deindustrialisation had left deep scars on a large number of communities nationwide. Over 13 years Labour in government did much to address the underlying issues those communities faced, but that change was never secured and so following the 2008 capitalist crash, and the subsequent decade of austerity, those communities fell behind again. The hollowing out they experienced in the 2010s echoed that of the 1980s and was a reminder of how the affluent parts of the UK had left them far behind. From seaside towns to small former industrial towns in the midlands, to Yorkshire and Lancashire and the north and southwest; while London boomed these communities looked on at investment flowing away from them. In 2019 the Conservatives promised much as Labour did in 1997 to redress the balance of investment, but following COVID the economic world will look very different.

In calling for a renewal of Liberal Democracy the substance of economic regeneration must be found in an environmentally sustainable future based on skills and education, entrepreneurial enterprise backed by infrastructural investment alongside a realignment that sees money flow into communities like our seaside towns and small former industrial communities. Coupled with subsidiarity and a growth of local government, central government must become the enabler not the doer. It has to be that central government sees its role as the link in the chain between new centres of power devolved around the country.

Many politicians talk about a 'green new deal', it is fast becoming a progressive mainstream policy commitment. The New Economics Foundation says:

> "Back in 2008, NEF was part of a visionary group that proposed a Green New Deal. Now the school strikers, Extinction Rebellion and politicians like Alexandria Ocasio-Cortez have combined with influential reports from the Committee on Climate Change and the Intergovernmental Panel on Climate Change to thrust climate and the Green New Deal back up the political agenda. They have forced political parties into competing on carbon targets." [45]

There is a fundamental challenge between policy in opposition and policy in government for proponents of Liberal Democracy. The issue for the proponents of the 'green new deal' is that it cannot simply be a set of policies or a chapter of a manifesto. Like Universal Human Rights or the Rule of Law we need to see the commitment to environmentalism become a core principle of Liberal Democracy.

The editorial in the Guardian on the 12th May 2019 said:

> "The Green New Deal is probably the most fashionable policy in the English-speaking world. In Britain it is advocated by both Tory MPs and Jeremy Corbyn; while a non-partisan

---

[45] https://neweconomics.org/about/our-missions/green-new-deal accessed on 30th July 2020.

Canadian coalition of nearly 70 groups are backing such a scheme. However, it has been made flesh by US Democrats, in particular the political phenomenon in the US House of Representatives, Alexandria Ocasio-Cortez. Ms Ocasio-Cortez has spelled out what a Green New Deal involves in a House resolution: rejecting economic orthodoxy to confront climate change."[46]

In many ways this economic pillar of renewal is the most important because it concerns the most tangible aspect of people's lives and that will make a difference and pull the rug from under the populists who prey on the economic disadvantage lived by so many. Populists promote a 'culture war' of identity, blaming others for people's woes. They lack credible economic answers, and in that vacuum the proponents of Liberal Democracy have an opportunity to play their trump card, investment and economic growth that lifts people out of their condition and offers hope.

The rich tradition of Liberal economic thought that has manifested itself in the twentieth century in Western governments of all complexions, from Keynes to Friedman, and was unleashed in a pure neoliberal form in the 1970s and 1980s, all founded in market capitalism, is out of date when we consider the new reality of climate change. The worldwide environmental disaster is here now because of the current global capitalist economic model. At this macrolevel the strategic shift required to a new economic model is fundamental, but the impact of that shift on the world economy needs new thinking because the consequences for livelihoods and poverty are equally profound.

---

[46] https://www.theguardian.com/commentisfree/2019/may/12/the-guardian-view-on-a-green-new-deal-we-need-it-now accessed on 30th July 2020.

Growth based on GDP and sustained by market capitalism based on the fossil fuels model will result in climate change which will devastate the planet. Thus, there is no choice, only denial. If those vested interests in the corporatist capitalist elite continue to protect their position by denying climate change and preventing transformation, supported by their populist allies, they condemn the rest of us and themselves.

Again, we could expend huge energy and resources seeking a revolution to bring these corporatists down, but it will fail and people are just not interested in such modern revolutions. People want politics that answers their economic problems, they want to see tangible change they can understand and touch. The post-covid world will need far more than idealism it needs realist perspectives focused on strong value-based foundations. The economic policies need to derive from a thorough appreciation of the societal impact of covid and its economic consequences.

Proponents of Liberal Democracy need to embrace realism to address climate change, but also tackle poverty and a new economic model to address the post-covid world. It is a brave new politics and because of that it needs grounding in people's lives. Unless the masses buy into change, it will only be a lofty ideal talked of by the chattering classes. Again, leadership needs to mould a new consensus.

The argument in the 2019 General Election about nationalising the railways and public utilities had widespread public support, but people did not vote for those policies because they did not believe they could be delivered. This disconnect is the key link any renewal of Liberal Democracy has to address. People need to believe their prosperity and economic security can be delivered through the change proposed. This is no easy feat to achieve set against the populists' siren voices of economic nationalism and climate change denial. In each of the progressive landslide victories in 1906, 1945, 1966 and 1997 the population bought into the message of change.

From a long-term perspective, proponents of Liberal Democracy need to find consensus that promotes change over a period which will cement such transformation. There is a need in the first instance to address the challenge of poverty and investment as a priority, and set in place the building blocks for economic transformation to address climate change.

This is not a zero-sum game; a lot of work has been done in part which needs knitting together into a coherent approach. For example, the reliance on coal energy has been broken in the UK and there is a growing renewables industry, that is a point for continued and enhanced investment. There is a need for a long-term economic strategy with essential waypoints which meet people's expectations. People need to see and be able to touch the change that they are a part of. Confidence is key and again this is a battle for hearts and minds.

Throughout the 1980s Labour shifted its policy positions to accept in principle the economic changes of the decade brought about by the neoliberals. They succumbed to the structural changes in the economy and in society. Under Blair there was no rowing back to the 1970s. Equally now any renewal of Liberal Democracy for the 2020s must not look back, it has to boldly address the future and paint the tangible picture people can see and touch.

People want jobs, which pay well and enable them to keep their families secure. They want a home as well as lives that are fulfilling and education for their children that means the future is better for the next generation. People want these tangible economic opportunities, proponents of Liberal Democracy must ensure they won't cost the earth.

Environmental Sustainability

"Right now, we are facing a manmade disaster of global scale, our greatest threat in thousands of years: climate change. If we don't take action, the collapse of our civilisations and the extinction of much of the natural world is on the horizon." – Sir David Attenborough at the UN Climate Change Summit, Poland, 2018. [47]

There is no point to anything written here, there is no point to renewing Liberal Democracy, if the planet is ravaged by manmade climate change. This is perhaps the singular biggest dividing line between the populists and proponents of Liberal Democracy. Climate change deniers or excusers are leading the dismantling of the good work achieved by so many before them and endangering the world on the back of their nationalist and individualist agenda. Their attitude of 'sod' the rest of the world and its future, to them the only thing that matters is their core support. Their approach in power literally casts the rest of us adrift.

Their ascendency comes at the world's most vulnerable moment, because unless change is achieved in only a very

---

[47] https://www.bbc.co.uk/news/science-environment-46398057 accessed on 30th July 2020.

few years' time, the damage will be irreversible. Their short-termism condemns future generations. But why does that surprise us. Old white men in positions of power dictating to the world their narrow populist agenda has played on people's fears and they are in control. Any renewal of Liberal Democracy that seeks to change this has to address climate change directly as a fundamental principle not a policy addition to a manifesto. We must understand that the issue runs to the heart of how we would organise future society.

It is as fundamental a question as that. Economically, socially, politically and philosophically our species' future rests on whether the proponents of Liberal Democracy can rest control from the populists and bring new policy forward which actually delivers change to address the climate crisis. It really doesn't get any bigger or more fundamental than that, the fight is for the future of the planet and it is not dramatic to say so.

If those who worry about immigration or feel disconnected from globalisation don't understand now that we are connected by the planet we live on, then the proponents of Liberal Democracy need to vigorously help them see the light. The only way to do this is to make the impact of climate change tangible to their lives. Floods, hurricanes, storms and all forms of extreme weather; food shortages; pandemics all stem from the same source and that is manmade climate change and the impact we have as a species on the natural world.

> *"Right now, we are facing a manmade disaster of global scale, our greatest threat in thousands of years: climate change. If we don't take action, the collapse of our civilisations and the*

*extinction of much of the natural world is on the horizon."
"The moment of crisis has come, we can no longer prevari-
cate."* – Sir David Attenborough, BBC, January 2020. [48]

The sixth and final pillar of renewal for Liberal Democracy
must be a cast-iron guarantee that as with the fundamental
philosophical underpinnings of universal human rights, or
democracy, or the rule of law, tackling climate change must
become a central tenet of Liberal Democracy. The idea of
the 'Good Society' must become the 'Good Green Society'.

Broadening this debate while we counter the false narratives
of nationalism through an assertion of environmentalism
as a tenet of Liberal Democracy, lets actually look towards
the people who really need that liberty and representation.
Often decolonialising is the best way to reverse this process,
allowing those who have maintained the lands for untold
generations to have their lands back.

The lives of the indigenous people of the Amazon would be
protected by the same rights that would protect the Amazon
itself. Similarly, the rights of the indigenous peoples of
Bolivia, India, Canada, Australia, New Zealand, Hawaii,
America and the thousands of tribes, nations and peoples
that are not represented, all of them and all of their rights
are protections for the environment. Anti-imperialism is
not a niche focus of the far left, it is a good place to start
with environmentalism.

Investing in greener forms of development is also good, not
just here but in other countries. Say what you want about

_____

[48] https://www.independent.co.uk/environment/david-attenborough-
climate-change-crisis-bbc-global-warming-a9286036.html accessed on
30th July 2020.

China's presence in Africa, and it is as imperialist as the 'West', the high-speed railways they are investing in are a form of green infrastructure that not only allows countries to develop but, in some ways, to supersede the non-green areas of industrialisation. Imagine what could be achieved if Britain actually worked to reduce desertification, clean the oceans and cut down on meat products? The main issue with environmentalism is that it is seen as a sacrifice for a later benefit.

The protests led by children are profoundly inspirational, because this issue speaks to their future more than any other principle we have discussed. Older generations are not as easily willing to change their lives in the numbers required to achieve the revolutionary change required given the level of crisis we see. Politicians have failed to lead, they've moved slowly and with resistance to more radical policy, but as time runs out because the tipping point of no return gets closer the danger that point poses grows greater in people's minds.

The London Economic published an article in January 2020 before covid where they said: *"The iconic Doomsday Clock symbolizing the gravest perils facing humankind is now closer to midnight than at any point since its creation in 1947. The clock, which serves as a metaphor for global apocalypse, was moved forward by 20 seconds."*[49]

Rachel Bronson, president and chief executive of the *Bulletin of the Atomic Scientists*, which sets the reading, said in the article:

---

[49] https://www.thelondoneconomic.com/news/world-news/doomsday-clock-moves-closer-to-midnight-and-global-apocalypse-than-ever/23/01 accessed on 30th July 2020.

"The world has entered into the realm of a two-minute warning, a period when danger is high and the margin for error low. It is 100 seconds to midnight. We are now expressing how close the world is to catastrophe in seconds – not hours, or even minutes. It is the closest to Doomsday we have ever been in the history of the Doomsday Clock. We now face a true emergency – an absolutely unacceptable state of world affairs that has eliminated any margin for error or further delay."[50]

Our species future rests on how serious we really are about changing society, our economy, our lives to tackle climate change, it is therefore critical that Environmental Sustainability becomes a tenet of Liberal Democracy.

---

[50] Ibid. https://www.thelondoneconomic.com

Conclusion:
The Future of Liberal Democracy

"There is also an internal challenge to liberal democracy—a challenge from populists who seek to drive a wedge between democracy and liberalism. Liberal norms and policies, they claim, weaken democracy and harm the people." William Galston, 2018 [51]

This analysis has attempted to unpack a series of pillars or building blocks on which we might construct a new Liberal Democratic Grand Strategy. The policies that fall out of the debate about these fundamental building blocks will be essential to any success proponents of Liberal Democracy have in pushing back against the populists. As our argument has progressed we have alluded to a few possible policies that naturally, we suggest, fall out of the principle building blocks explored here.

It is reasonable to say that the Liberal political spectrum is as broad as the right and left of the political spectrum and in this analysis, we have gravitated to the centre left. It is my contention that the modern political climate needs a strong centre left to counter the rise of the far right, Alt-Right and

---

[51] https://www.brookings.edu/research/the-populist-challenge-to-liberal-democracy/ accessed on 30th July 2020.

populists. That strength can and should be drawn from the rich history of Liberal Democratic principles we have explored here. It is not an exhaustive list. It is not a manifesto and it should not be read as such. It is meant as an analysis of grand strategic principles designed to underpin a renewal of Liberal Democracy.

When I talk to people about politics there is a sense that politics means little to them, but they are angry at the way politics and politicians have let them down. People want to feel politics has value, that if they vote or participate it will make a difference. If the institutions of the Liberal Democratic system fail them then why would they not lose confidence and turn to the populists?

The left has failed to offer a meaningful, believable alternative and in that space the populists and far-right have run riot with such major transformations as Brexit and the Trump election victory in 2016.

The documents we have referred to here in this paper are in-themselves a distraction from the ideas they contain. Any renewal must focus on these ideas as the basis for regeneration. It is reasonable to develop a new Magna Carta that embraces the Rule of Law, a new Declaration of Rights that secures individual liberty, a new localism that devolves democracy.

The documents are limited to the time and context in which they were prepared and so they reflect for example a Bill of Rights that were not universal but limited to white men of a certain age. The Magna Carta was not for 'all free men', it was again limited by the revisions of the writers in 1225 to a list of the worthiest. It is the profound and relevant ideas contained in these documents that need modern interpretation and articulation. We should use that rich history to renew our future.

In devolving democracy, it is a fundamental question of how far do you go? Do we take the principle of subsidiarity into the boardroom? How do people exercise localism in their lives? More than the boardroom, how do people engage with a form of capitalism that's serves their interests, not the interests of capitalism itself. How do we democratise capitalism?

Democracy is not simply about voting, it is about participation and representation that ensures effective engagement. In promoting the democratisation of capitalism, the proponents of Liberal Democracy could and should encourage a direct assault on the concentration of power in corporate giants like Amazon or Google. But, they do this by connecting these ideals to the real lives of people.

We need to affirm a new consensus of these principles in order that politics itself is changed and policies that fall out of these principles fulfil the aims and objectives of this grand strategy.

Looking forward for a positive alternative this analysis suggests that a renewal of Liberal Democracy based on the six principles espoused here could reinvigorate the centre left of politics at least in the UK. Let's lay a new Liberal Democratic foundation fit for the 2020s and beyond:

1. The Rule of Law
2. Democracy and Subsidiarity
3. Universal Human Rights

4. Social Justice and Equality
5. Economic Security and Opportunity
6. Environmental Sustainability

There is much at stake, not least the future of Western Democracy, let us not fool ourselves. The likes of Trump and Johnson, ably abetted by their lieutenants, have undermined the principles of our democracy. They are not Conservatives, they are populists and they are dangerous. The threat they pose to democracy is deep and serious. That is why proponents of Liberal Democracy have got to step up and meet the challenge. Which must be through substance and principle that offers something real to people, something people can touch as a part of their lives.

We must shine a light of principle on a future that can improve people's lives and deliver progress, which offers hope, that can lift our politics to again be worthy of the true power of Liberal Democracy.

> *"The current ills of liberal democracy are deep and pervasive. Surmounting them will require intellectual clarity and political leaders who are willing to take risks to serve the long-term interests of their countries. Human choice, not historical inevitability, will determine liberal democracy's fate."* – William Galston, 2018 [52]

---

[52] https://www.brookings.edu/research/the-populist-challenge-to-liberal-democracy/ accessed on 30th July 2020.

CPSIA information can be obtained
at www.ICGtesting.com
Printed in the USA
LVHW031116010321
680247LV00002B/395